#1 Best Selling Book

Thank you Launch Team for helping me get to #1.

Thousands sold!

Book Launch Stats

#1 Children's Book Social Emotional Issues

#1 Children's Book Leadership

#1 Teen Book Social Emotional Issues

#1 Children's Book on Friendships

#23 Motivational Book All Ages

Top Rated Student Leadership Book 40+ 5 Star Reviews

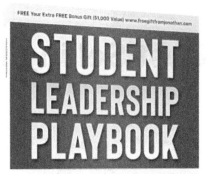

Join the Student Leadership Success Challenge!
$100 FREE!

READ THIS FIRST

Just to say thanks for buying my book, I would like to give you the Challenge 100% FREE!

Get Certificate of completion for Resume!

TO DOWNLOAD GO TO:
www.FreeGiftFromJonathan.com

SPECIAL ~~$1000~~ <u>FREE</u> BONUS GIFT FOR <u>YOU</u>!

To help you achieve more success, there are **FREE BONUS RESOURCES** for you at:

Get your 8 <u>FREE</u> in-depth training videos sharing

- How top achieving student leaders
- Attract more followers!
- Increase influence!
- Lead & Achieve more Goals!
- Create Movements & Go Viral!
- Plus Secret Bonuses.

www.FreeGiftFromJonathan.com

THE IDEAL PROFESSIONAL SPEAKER FOR YOUR NEXT EVENT!

TO CONTACT OR BOOK JONATHAN TO SPEAK:
(832) 713-0296
jonathan@jmedinaspeaks.com
topcollegespeaker.com

Praise for Jonathan Medina "America's #1 Youth Motivator"

Eric Thomas

& Associates President Carlos "CJ" Quinney

"Jonathan's Keynote is one of my FAVORITE! Funny! Energetic! Super IMPACTFUL… Gamechanger making moves all over the world"

⭐ ⭐ ⭐ ⭐ ⭐

Joe Theismann NFL MVP, Superbowl Champion, Heisman Finalist, NFL Broadcaster & Celebrity Speaker

"OH SHOOT! AMAZING!"

Kevin Harrington Original Shark on Shark Tank
Founder of As Seen on TV & Celebrity Speaker

"That was Freakin Awesome! WOW!"

Les Brown- Top 5 Motivational Speaker All Time

"Jonathan Medina is Greatness"

#GEARUPworks
Look at all the 5 Star Reviews

 Diane

★★★★★ **Great leadership Resource**
Reviewed in the United States on August 26, 2020
Verified Purchase

Love the way the author references his personal life moving through school and various groups he had the chance to be a part of, even if not in a leadership role.
Lot of catch phrases, commitment equals success; it's not where you start but where you finish; reference to coaching and learning the playbook; small changes can make huge impacts.
Chapter One focuses on Goals - love the quotes included in the chapter on goals; makes it personal; and resources are included in the chapter to make it almost like a workbook that you can use to create and track your own goals.
True story, I was intentionally going to the gym after reading the chapter and it made me want to set higher goals for myself at the gym.
Finally, love the acronym for the chapters - GAME TIME - Goals, Attitude, Mindset, Embody and Teamwork, Invest, Measure, and Engage.
I think the author is providing our youth with information and great resource to help them become leaders.

Melissa Lopez National GEAR UP Advisory Commision & Region 1 Director
"Jonathan BLEW EVERYONE AWAY!! Just AMAZING! CONNECTED! ★★★★★

"Jonathan's story is powerful. I would recommend Jonathan because we still have a lot of students just like Jonathan. I was one of them." **-Joel UMD** ★★★★★

"Jonathan's personal stories were the **best**. So many of our students have similar stories." **Betsy Lumley VSU** ★★★★★

"My favorite part was your perseverance and how you inspire your brother to succeed." ★★★★★ **Vivian West Virginia University**

Sofia Pena UTRGV GEAR UP Director ★★★★ "He **relates** to our students, the students relate to him. He is the **best motivator we have ever had**"

#TRIOworks

Veronica Silva- Texas A&M Kingsville TRIO Director SSS & Talent Search

"**WOWWWWWW WHAT AN UPLIFTING PRESENTATION**! The entire presentation was most uplifting. I would highly **RECOMMEND** Jonathan for any TRIO program that serves first generation and low income students (College, High School, and Junior High Students), because Jonathan is a prime example of "you have the burning desire to achieve, you can, despite the odds!"- **Lila Love Director Federal TRIO Upward Bound Old Dominion University** ★ ★ ★ ★ ★

"The Lively engagement was key. You are the real deal, genuine and passionate. You shared your heart with us, the participants. That makes the message memorable. I had so much fun. " ★ ★ ★ ★ ★ **Prof Kim Shelton Mansfield University** TRIO

"I lived hearing Jonathan's story and the audience interaction. Our program is located in rural SW VA, so I know a lot of our students could relate to your experiences." **Christy MECC** ★ ★ ★ ★ ★

"We work with mostly first generation students who experience some of the same obstacles as Jonathan did. I can't wait to share Jonathan's story of how to persevere." Djenaba Bahar ★ ★ ★ ★ ★

TABLE OF CONTENTS

Introduction to Student Leadership 5 C's 1

Section 1/ First Half Lead Yourself

CHAPTER 1 Student Leadership GOALS 14

CHAPTER 2 Student Leadership ATTITUDE 21

CHAPTER 3 Student Leadership MINDSET 29

CHAPTER 4 Student Leadership EMBODY 38

Section 2/ Second Half Leading Others

CHAPTER 5 Student Leadership TEAMWORK 44

CHAPTER 6 Student Leadership INVEST 53

CHAPTER 7 Student Leadership MEASURE 61

CHAPTER 8 Student Leadership ENGAGE 70

LEADERSHIP NOTES 87

Book Launch Stats 89

# INTRODUCTION TO STUDENT LEADERSHIP 5 C'S

CHOOSE to attend, join, and be a part of the club, organization, team, etc. The first step is always the hardest. I can remember starting middle school and seeing signs/flyers on the walls. Come to this meeting. Join our club. Be a part of our organization.

I would look at those signs in the hallways and think to myself I want to attend the meeting. I would be handed a flyer and asked to join the club but the voice in my head would start to tell me that I would not fit in. The voice in my head would tell me that they would not want me in the club. The voice in my head would tell me I was not good enough to be a part of the club, organization or team.

After I made the choice to not go to the meeting I would walk by the signs and feel ashamed. After I didn't join the club, I felt like a coward. After I didn't become a part of the organization/team, I felt like a loser.

I wanted so badly to feel like a winner. I wanted so badly to feel the excitement from attending the meetings. I wanted to feel the unity in joining the clubs and organizations. I wanted to feel the intense nervousness/confidence of being on the team. I wanted so bad to feel a part of something bigger than myself. I wanted to become something bigger than myself.

That was sixth grade. A year later, in seventh grade, I walked down the halls of a different school. I had moved but I would still see the signs on the walls. I was older, taller, and had more pimples, but the students still handed me flyers to join the clubs. I was stronger and faster (still weak - but not *as* weak, still slow - but not *as* slow) and even more, they asked me to be a part of the teams. Not only did the same experience follow me, but the same feelings followed me. The voice in my head followed me. The burning desire on the inside followed me.

Would anything be different in seventh grade or would I still feel ashamed, feel like a coward, feel like a loser?

Seventhgrade was so much different because **I made a choice.** Whatever grade you are in, **you can make a choice.** I did not let the voice in my head make the choice for me. I made the choice to attend, join, and be a part my seventh grade year. I made the choice to attend the meetings I saw on the wall. I made a choice to join the clubs and organizations. I made a choice to be a part of the team. I made the choice to be a part of something bigger than myself. I made a choice to become something bigger than myself.

COMMIT to becoming a student leader. When I first joined all the clubs,organizations, groups and teams, I was not what some people describe as a natural leader. I was not very good at contributing as a member of the clubs, groups, organizations, and teams. Just like I mentioned before, I began to join many clubs, organizations, groups, and teams. I joined the chess club and began to play chess every Wednesday after school. I competed in UIL which are academic competitions. I joined the football team, which I had wanted to do since I was very young. I joined the basketball team. I joined track.

I was not an officer in any of the clubs, organizations, groups, or teams. I was not elected to be a leader. I was not selected to be a leader. I was just happy to be a member. I was just happy to be a teammate. I was happy to be a part or piece.

The world will try to tell you that leaders are born. The world will try to tell you that you either have "it" or you do not have "it". Perhaps some of us are born with "it". What is "it"? Perhaps they mean some leadership gene. Perhaps they mean some leadership gift. Perhaps they mean something unexplainable. Whatever the "it" is, I did not have "it" when I joined the clubs.

Can you relate to feeling like you don't have "it"? Do you feel like you have "it" already?

Whether you feel you have "it" or not, you need to make a **COMMITMENT** to leadership.

I remember feeling very *disappointed* when I made the B team in football. I remember feeling *discouraged* when I would lose in chess competitions. I remember feeling *deflated* when I thought I was good at basketball but again made the B team.

Then my coach told me something that changed my life. My coach told me, **"It's not where you start, but where you finish."**

I watched as the student leaders would achieve success in our clubs. I watched as the student leaders would achieve success as an individual. I watched as the student leaders would win awards. I watched as student leaders became the stars. I watched as student leaders made our clubs, organizations, and teams successful.

What I observed most was that the best student leaders committed to being student leaders. The best student leaders committed to being successful. The best student leaders were committed even when the teacher, sponsor, and coach was not looking. The most committed student leaders always seemed to become the most successful.

Colleges, Universities, Scholarships, and Jobs all are looking for committed student leaders. When I was applying to colleges, every application had a section asking me if I was a part of any student leadership organizations. The applications asked if I had been part of teams. Then they all had a section that asked if I was a leader. I saw my friends' applications. Some had a lot to write about in those applications, but some left the sections on student leadership blank. I applied for elite scholarships and they asked the same kind of questions. Those students who had committed to being student leaders were accepted to the elite schools. Those students who had committed to being student leaders received the most scholarships. Those students who had committed to being student leaders got the best jobs after school.

Because I did not naturally have the "it" factor in my student leadership I spent many many hours observing the successful student leaders looking for the playbook of success. I found that commitment levels equaled success levels. I made the decision that I needed to be committed if I wanted to be successful. Because I made a commitment to be a leader, I began to do the things that student leaders do. I committed to work harder and to do more. I committed to becoming more. I committed to becoming a student leader. **You** must **commit** to being a student leader.

COACHING. Learn the PLAYBOOK. In first to third grade, a group of us that got to school before the other students would play outside. We would stand on the edge of the concrete and race each other to the fence. I am proud to say that in first grade I was the fastest. But by second grade I was not anymore. By the time I was in ninth grade I was down to about the middle of the pack. It seemed like everyone around me was getting faster and I was staying the same.

Have you ever felt like everyone is improving and you are staying the same?

Coach De La Rosa saw me running one day and told me the secret to how I could instantly increase my speed. After learning the secret, I was one of the fastest runners on my football team despite being much larger than all of the other fast runners. The trick he showed me made me fast enough to start getting attention from universities. The trick he showed me moved me from the back of the line to the front of each race.

What was the huge change that made me 2x, 3x, 10x faster? I had been running on my heels and he told me to run on the balls of my feet instead when I was trying to run full speed. It was not a huge change, but rather a small change but with a huge impact. That small shift in moving from heel to the ball of my feet was a game changer. Even after my environment changed because of different sports or seasons, the change helped in all environments. I was running outside, inside, on tracks, grass, and wood indoor gyms, but my speed did not change as much compared to the difference from the change I made from my coaches tip.

Did you know that as a student leader you can make many small changes or shifts that can have a huge impact on *your* results?

The same way the rest of my body shifted when I moved the weight/force from my heels to the balls of my feet, when you improve as a student leader, the entire weight and force of the organization, group, team that you lead will change.

An improving leader improves an entire organization, group, or team just like a rising tide lifts all boats.

My student leadership coaches helped me learn to speak in public and have confidence as a speaker. They helped me become a clear communicator. They helped me become persuasive to inspire my peers. My student leadership coaches helped me to go from starting a new club to it being one of the largest clubs on campus. The shifts, changes, and improvements that my coaches helped me with made me successful. It was all because of the coaches. I could use confidence and public speaking everywhere.

I join or start new clubs, but while the club was new the previous advice from my coach would help me in the new environment. All the way to this day when I am on stage or when I am interacting with different teams. Everything I do now is a result of the good coaching I had as a student leader. You can have your entire life become better by listening to the good advice of the proper coaches.

My college admissions coach helped me change my personal statement college essay, taking it from okay to one that got me into the most prestigious schools. My college admissions coach helped me to prepare my application, taking it from good to great. Then I had a career coach help me to get my first job and helped me to be successful in my roles.

Oftentimes my coaches helped me correct mistakes that I had been making for years. They helped me see mistakes that I could not see. They helped me become the leader I needed to become to lead effectively.

This book is not for student leaders not willing to be coached. You can be a great student leader, but being a great student leader means that you will need to be coached to correct mistakes and make improvements. Are you ready? Are you willing? Are you **coachable**?

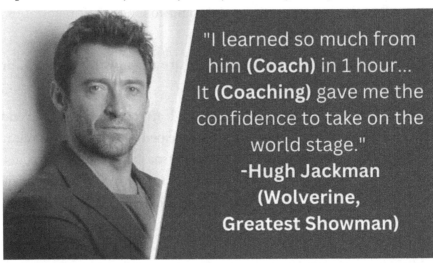

"I learned so much from him **(Coach)** in 1 hour... It **(Coaching)** gave me the confidence to take on the world stage."
-Hugh Jackman
(Wolverine, Greatest Showman)

COMMUNITY. We are in this TOGETHER. As a student leader, I will never forget the summer I spent with a program called the Leadership Enterprise for a Diverse America. Fifty Five or so students from across the United States were brought together in a cohort of Student Leaders for this special program at Princeton University. I had never been on a plane before and I was a bit nervous about giving up my summer. We spent all summer learning together. We spent all summer being challenged together. We spent all summer growing as leaders together. We became a community of like minded leaders. We all left that summer a community believing that we could go and change the world. We started that summer believing we could apply to highly selective schools, but we ended that summer believing we could be **accepted** and attend our dream schools. We left that summer believing we could change ourselves, our families, our communities, and the world.

Eight weeks later we all had to get on a plane, say goodbye, and go to change the world alone. The group that I bonded with all summer with was ending. On the same mission but no longer together physically.

Social media changed our ability to connect and stay a strong community. Before we would have only had emailing and phone calls to communicate with one another. But before we left that summer many of us learned about this new thing called social media. What critical tool did we use to stay together on the mission to change ourselves, our family, our community? We used the critical tool called MySpace. I know none of you probably know what this social network was, but this platform came out before facebook or when facebook was only for college students.

Because of social media we could continue to learn together. We could continue to challenge ourselves together. We could encourage each other to apply to highly selective schools together. We could believe together. We could Dream together. WE could change ourselves, our families, our community, and the world together.

As I travel the country speaking with students, many tell me that they feel alone. Nobody to learn with. Nobody to challenge each other with. Nobody to be on the journey with them. Because of that we have created a **Exclusive Private Group** for students ready to learn together. Student Leaders ready to be challenged together. Student Leaders ready to grow together. Student Leaders ready to change themselves, their family, their community, and the world TOGETHER.

https://www.facebook.com/groups/studentleadershipchampions

Or scan the QR Code Below to Join the Exclusive FB Group

By purchasing this book you have Joined the Exclusive Private Group/COMMUNITY of students coming TOGETHER. Join our exclusive facebook group/COMMUNITY for Student Leaders. Facebook Lives with new tips on how to be a Successful Student Leader & Success Student. Special training on how to get Accepted to Top Colleges & Win Top Scholarships. Network with other Student Leaders from across the country to grow as student leaders together.

Would CHOOSING to join a club, organization, team be helpful? YES!

Would COMMITTING to becoming a student leader be helpful? YES!

Would COACHING help you with the step by step process of student leadership be helpful? YES!

Would a COMMUNITY of other student leaders worldwide be helpful in your journey in student leadership? YES!

Can I offer you something special so you can CREATE and win at being a student leader? YES!

Create your Future! My high school coach gave me a book and told me if I read the book everyday it would teach me to create my future. It would teach me to create better opportunities for my family. My coach gifted me the book that would create a better leader in me. The gift helped me to influence all my success. **Gift this book to a student leader and help them create a better world.**

This book and program are for student leaders who are serious. This is for the student leaders that want to win. This is for the student leaders who want to create a movement. This is for the student leaders who are willing to change the world.

If you are not serious about being a true student leader this next part is not for you. If you are not interested in being the kind of student leader that leads others and makes an impact on the world this is not for you. If you are not a student leader interested in joining a movement this is not for you. Put the book down and walk away.

For those of you still here.

CONGRATS on being the new breed of student leader. I will share 1 Special Bonus Gift at the end of this book. But you have to act now. Start reading each chapter and implementing the secret playbook for Student Leadership Success.

topschoolspeakers.com

NOTES

topschoolspeakers.com

Scan the QR Code to Become a Certified Student Leader

CHAPTER 1
STUDENT LEADERSHIP GOALS

Jonathan Medina "What size <u>GOALS</u> do you have? Student Leaders DREAM BIG!"

Without visions, goals, and dreams students quit, lose, and fail. Student Leaders need to have Goals and Dreams because they have impact and influence on the entire campus. The other students in your school need you to help share your Vision. The other students in your organizations need you to help find Goals. The other students on your teams need you to help them Dream.

14 |

As I travel the country speaking at schools as a top youth speaker to motivate students, many students ask to take selfies or they connect with me on instagram @jmedinaspeaks. While taking the photos or reading comments I always ask students what they want to be when they grow up. Many students look me in the eye or the message me on instragram and say they don't know what they want to be when they grow up. They don't have long term *Goals*. They don't have *Dreams* of the future.

Fun Fact: We will all (100%) be somewhere 1 yr, 5 yrs, 10 yrs, 20 yrs from now.

Dr. Martin Luther King "I had a _____" *DREAM!*

Dr. Martin Luther King had a dream, but it was not for himself. He had a dream that would change the world. He had a dream that would make the world a better place for all of us. Dr. Martin Luther King shared his dream and now we get to experience a better world.

Hellen Keller "The only thing worse than being blind is having sight but no *VISION*"

VISION definition: Ability to plan, think, & forecast future with imagination, wisdom, & growth in mind.

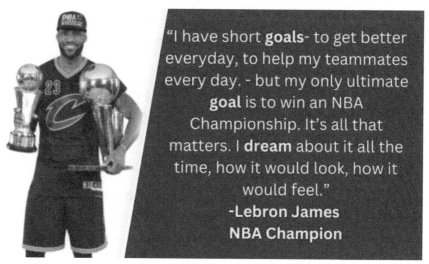

"I have short **goals**- to get better everyday, to help my teammates every day. - but my only ultimate **goal** is to win an NBA Championship. It's all that matters. I **dream** about it all the time, how it would look, how it would feel."
-Lebron James
NBA Champion

Playbook

Lebron James, "I have short goals- to get better everyday, to help my teammates every day. - but my only ultimate goal is to win an NBA Championship. It's all that matters. I dream about it all the time, how it would look, how it would feel."

I am a big Lebron James fan and I know he has a **BIG OLD GOAL (BOG)** of being the greatest Basketball Player of all time. I also love the fact that his goals include helping his teammates. Make sure to keep in mind that your goals should include how you are helping the others in your group, organization, and team.

When I was a young student I remember making goals that someday I would be a good athlete. Some day BIG OLD Goals, I would play Varsity Football & Basketball. Big OLD Goals that my grades would be at the top of the class. BIG OLD GOALS, I would have lots of friends. *Big OLD GOALS* I would get offers to play for Division 1 schools. Big Old Goals.

As a student leader you need to make goals that can inspire, motivate, and lead the organization you are a member of or leading. As a student leader you need to identify and write down your everyday goals. Lebron has goals of getting better every day and helping his teammates get better everyday. How can you grow as a leader everyday and help the organization or team grow everyday?

As a student leader what are the big ultimate goals that you have? What is your Championship?

Lebron James

BOG BIG OLD GOAL= Greatest Basketball player of all time Ultimate Goal or

Year Goal= Win NBA Championship

Daily Goal = Get Better, Help teammates get better

Start with BIG OLD GOAL. Next This Year Goals to get to BOG Today Goals Dream how it will look, feel, taste.

Student Leader (Write Your Name Here _____)

What is your BOG BIG OLD GOAL? _____

What is your Year Goal? _____

What is your Daily Goal? _____

How did you include your teammates into your Daily, Yearly, and Big Old Goals?

BIG OLD DREAM LONG TERM GOALS	1 YEAR GOAL
TODAY GOALS	HOW DOES IT LOOK? HOW DOES IT FEEL? HOW DOES IT TASTE? SMELL?

Homework/Overtime (Take Action)

1. On Sheet of Paper Make Quadrant & Fill it out.
2. Make a Decision to accomplish ALL Goals
3. Take Action & Complete all of your Daily Goals
4. Take a picture of your Quadrant and tag me on Instagram @jmedinaspeaks

STUDENT LEADERS SET BIG GOALS!
STUDENT LEADERS SET BIG DREAMS!

Remember you are a Champion Student Leader. It's GAMETIME!

NOTES

topschoolspeakers.com

topschoolspeakers.com

Scan the QR Code to Become a Certified Student Leader

CHAPTER 2

STUDENT LEADERSHIP ATTITUDE

Jonathan Medina "ATTITUDE CHECK, TEAM COMES FIRST"

I recently did a survey on Instagram, Snapchat, TikTok, and Facebook. I asked my friends: *What is the hardest thing about working with kids these days?* I knew that many of my friends are student leadership advisors, sponsors, parents, educators, teachers, aunts, uncles, coaches.

The #1 response was "ATTITUDE"

As a student leader you set the attitude of everyone in the organization. When a student leader has a great attitude it will infect the other students because of the influence student leaders have. If you go to meetings, practice, competitions with a bad attitude, you are also giving everyone else in the group, organization, or team a bad attitude.

In high school I was captain of a highly successful basketball team. We went 3 rounds into the playoffs each year and were usually ranked top 3 in the area out of over 100 schools. Every-time we left on the road. Right as we exited the fence of the campus the entire bus would go quiet and I would stand up and yell...

ATTITUDE CHECK! And the rest of the team would yell **TEAM COMES FIRST. ATTITUDE CHECK! TEAM COMES FIRST! ATTITUDE CHECK! TEAM COMES FIRST!** We would do that 3 times.

We had to do this because my coach knew how important it was for our team success that we have a winning attitude. As captain, I understood that I had to be the biggest cheerleader for having a great attitude. As a student leader your responsibility is to create a winning attitude in your group, organization, and team.

Jackie Robinson, "A life is not important except the impact it has on other lives"

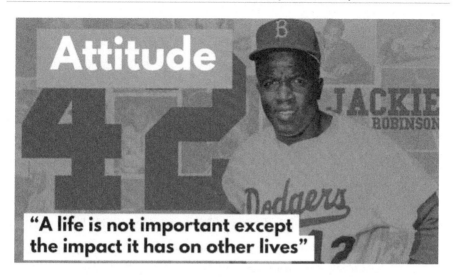

Jackie Robinson may have been one of the most impactful athletes in the history of sports. Did you watch the movie 42? Put the book down and go watch it if you have not. I love the attitude that Jackie Robinson had. He put a great deal of importance not on himself, but on others. That is the kind of attitude you must have as a Student Leader.

Winning Attitude: Team comes before you. Family comes before you. Others come before you. Say that out loud. "Team comes before me. Family comes before me. Others come before me."

- Who is counting on you to bring Winning Attitude?
- Who needs you to be a Champion Student Leader?

Write down 5-10 people that are counting on you? You need to write their actual name, you can put Mom next to name, but put actual names.

1.

2.

3.

4.

5.

My brother was an elite athlete. He was an All-American and won a championship while in school. I am jealous of the huge ring. Don't tell him. His senior year he was a part of a pro day. A ton of NFL Scouts came to my brothers university to watch him work out and do drills. Other players participated in hopes of being noticed by NFL Scouts and being offered a contract. It was a very special day. With all players and scouts watching my brother during his bench press (225 lbs for 40 repetitions) I stood on a bench to film over all the players and scouts. While filming my brother's agent asked if I was the older brother. He then told me how my brother told him that I had set a great example for him.

This was one of the coolest moments in my life. I love my family, especially little hermanito (brother). I was always trying to set a good example for my brother. I was hoping that my coach was correct about me learning to be a leader and my brother would learn to be a leader. My coach told me that if I would learn to be a leader on teams and organizations and I would learn to be a leader in my family.

I believed my brother was counting on me. Who is counting on you? I believed my family was counting on me. What organization or team is counting on you? When I wanted to quit, I would think my brother is counting on me. **ATTITUDE CHECK, TEAM COMES FIRST**. When I failed I had to keep trying because my brother was counting on me. **ATTITUDE CHECK, TEAM COMES FIRST.** When I was nervous about continuing my goals and dreams I would think to myself, my brother is counting on me. **ATTITUDE CHECK, TEAM COMES FIRST.**

- When you are putting others first, you create bigger meaning for your actions and goals. **Attitude Check**
- When your goals have an effect on others, they are better goals. **Attitude Check**
- When you don't stop because others are counting on you. **Attitude Check**
- When you show up to meetings, happy, prepared, and ready to win. **Attitude Check**

Homework/Overtime (Take Action)

Fill in the blanks below and post on instagram. Tag me, @jmedinaspeaks !

1. "I am (doing) _____ (your goal) for _____."

    Example: I am going to college for my family.

2. "I am sacrificing _____ for _____."

    Example: I am sacrificing my sleep to practice more for my team.

"GREAT Program, GREAT Speech" - Superintendent California

ATTITUDE CHECK: TEAM COMES FIRST FOR STUDENT LEADERS.

Remember you are a Champion Student Leader. It's GAMETIME!

NOTES

Scan the QR Code to Become a Certified Student Leader

CHAPTER 3
STUDENT LEADERSHIP MINDSET

Jonathan Medina "Winners never lose because they have a Winner's Mindset"

Student Leadership Winner's Mindset is important because so many students in your groups, organizations, clubs, and teams have never been shown how to have a winner's mindset. Student Leaders with a winner's mindset never lose because they learn from their failures. Student Leaders learn from their mistakes. Student Leaders never fail and quit. Student Leaders fail and keep trying. Student Leaders fail and keep growing. Student Leaders fail and get up again, and again, and again. Student Leaders keep learning, growing, and going until they learn to win. You need to show that mindset to all the other students that look are learning, watching, and being inspired by your example.

After one of my school assemblies a student came up to me and asked me, "Can I still go to college even if I failed one of my exams?" She was only in middle school. Of course she could overcome one failed exam in middle school, but she did make me think about how winners have a different mindset than losers. Harsh words maybe, but there is a big difference between the way people THINK. That's why it is so important for you as a student leader to show others how to have the mindset of a winner.

Student Athletes often ask me if they can go to college if they are on the b team in 7th, 8th, & 9th grade. I tell them about my experience in athletics. When I was in 7th grade I was so excited to join team sports. My mom never let me play football growing up even at the request of many of the other parents. I was bigger and faster in elementary. However, by the time I was in 7th grade I had become a husky young man. I was chubby or "Gordo". The school used the first week or two to have all the boys "try out" for the football team. I had no experience playing football with a helmet and pads. I was TERRIBLE. I was semi athletic, but was not used to the game at all. I was placed on the B team. B stands for BETTER. JK. B means I was not very good. I was ok. I did become a starter on the B team after all. I was very disappointed being on the B team. I wanted badly to be a good player but I did not experience success. I had a relative tell me that I was a loser, a failure and I would never be any good. My mindset was that I was too far behind and that I destined to be a B teamer. One day my coach told me something that changed my mindset.

7th grade coach "it's not where you start but where you FINISH!"

My coach was teaching me to have a Winners Mindset. Having a growth mindset is a big part of having a winners mindset. A growth mindset is when you believe things can change as opposed to having a fixed mindset as things won't change. A fixed mindset is when you believe you can't get smarter, learn a new way, get bigger, faster, stronger. Basically that you are stuck (Fixed).

Steph Curry, "We have to have the mentality that we have to work for everything we're going to get" Steph Curry understands what you as a student leader must understand. You will have to work to become a better leader. You will have to work to attract the help from others. You will have to work by reading and learning. You will have to work to become the best that you can be. You will have to work to win competitions. The mindset of working and getting better is what gives you the mindset of champions.

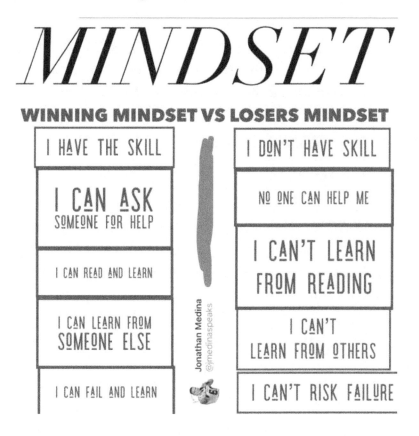

The Winner's mindset is to always look for a way to win and NEVER Quit!

As a student leader you may fail at something, but you must look for a way to win. You must figure out how to win somehow.

Maybe you are lacking skill. You may not be able to speak in public, but you can learn and practice. You may not be a very good writer, but you can learn to be a good writer. You may not be good at math, science, history, etc... but you can learn. You may not be able to dribble, shoot 3 point shots, or play defense, but you can learn. Maybe you don't know how to get a job, you can learn from others or by trying and eventually get one.

Maybe you need to join a better team or have people join your team. Doesn't have to be a sports team, but I mean ask someone to be helping you.

The internet is a wonderful thing and we read articles or books and learn how to win at something specific. We have books that can teach us how to make friends, how to get straight A's or how to get into selective colleges.

We can watch youtube videos and learn.

You can also try one way, then change something and try another way until you succeed.

Oprah, "Turn your wounds into wisdom"

Jonathan Medina "PUSH: Persevere Until Success Happens."

Whatever your goal is you must continue to Persevere Until Success Happens. Have the Champion Mindset as a Student Leader that you are going to PUSH.

Winners Mindset Method

1. Decide to NEVER Quit.

2. Find someone to help you figure it out.
3. Find someone to help you DO it.
4. Join someone who is succeeding at doing it.
5. Do some Research (Books, Internet, Youtube, Ask Friends)
6. Try Again, Try Again, Try Again,
7. PUSH: Persevere Until Success Happens

OVERTIME/Homework (Take Action)

Discussion Questions:

How old were you when you learned to walk? (may need to ask parents) _____

Did you get it the first time?

Did you ever fall learning to ride a bike, skate, skateboard, snowboard?

What is a goal that you failed at first then overcame? _____

Has someone ever helped you with a goal? _____

Have you ever used youtube to learn something? _____

STUDENT LEADERS LEARN TO WIN! STUDENT LEADERS HAVE A WINNERS MINDSET!

Remember you are a Champion Student Leader. It's GAMETIME!

NOTES

topschoolspeakers.com

Scan the QR Code to Become a Certified Student Leader

CHAPTER 4
STUDENT LEADERSHIP EMBODY

Jonathan Medina "As a student leader you should BE LEADERSHIP, DO LEADERSHIP, and THINK LEADERSHIP. As a Student Leader you must EMBODY Student Leadership."

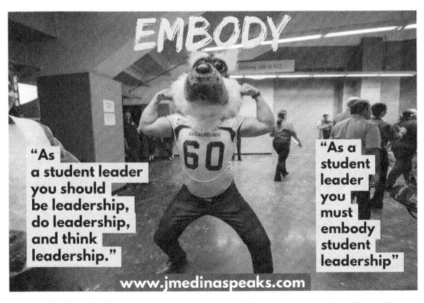

I love the level of importance Tom Brady puts on Embodying being a leader.

Tom Brady "When you're one of the leaders of the team, there are no days off."

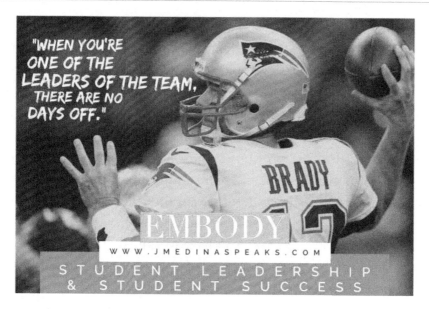

He says you must BE every single day. As a student leader you must realize that you have great influence. Those that are looking up to you are watching you. Some want to be just like you. Sometimes that can feel like a lot of pressure but I know that when you are focused on embodying they will follow you more. They will trust you more. They will support you more.

With Great Influence comes great responsibility. That is sort of stolen from one of the all time great movies. Spiderman.

Uncle Ben, "With great power comes Great Responsibility"

The number 35 is the greatest award anyone could receive at Georgetown University Football. 35 was given to the leader that Embodied the principles our coaches wanted us all to possess. This award comes from a great player that passed away inside the twin towers on Sept 11, 2001. While just about every 35 was a great leader, I will always remember this one game. I had a very difficult game because we were playing one of the best teams in the country. I think they even won the National Championship. I watched as #35 on my team took hit after hit. I still remember the sound of the collision. He kept getting up at sacrificing for the team. He kept getting up and pushing hard. He kept getting up and EMBODYING what it meant to be a leader. We drove down the field. We are down 3 and very little time left. We are going up the field but #35 is getting physically beat up. But he just continued to embody leadership play after play. Even when his back up offered to come in he decided to continue to take the punishment for the team. Just like the previous lesson. <u>Attitude Check team comes First</u>. We go down the field and score a touchdown and... We lost the game. I said we were down 3 but it was 3 touchdowns. Maybe more. But the point is that as a student leader you have to Embody the leadership position you have. You have to embody leadership even if you have not been elected or appointed because we all are leaders and we all have influence.

Overtime/Homework (Take Action)

1. What are the characteristics that you would want to embody as a student leader?
2. Who are some of the people that are seeing what you are doing?
3. Who are some people that you remember looking up to that Embodied characteristics of Leadership?

STUDENT LEADERS EMBODY STUDENT LEADERSHIP IN THEIR THOUGHTS, ACTIONS, AND DESTINY!

Remember you are a Champion Student Leader. It's GAMETIME!

NOTES

Scan the QR Code to Become a Certified Student Leader

CHAPTER 5

STUDENT LEADERSHIP TEAMWORK

Jonathan Medina -"You can only get so far alone. Teammates will take you to the top and keep you at the top."

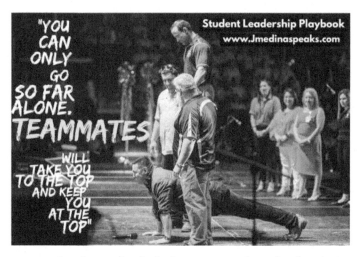

The reason having other's help as a student leader is important because others add so much to how effective you are. Sometimes it may feel like others slow us down as a student leader, but in the long run they will make us so much faster, better, and stronger.

As a student leader, it is important to have the help of others. The help of others will help us become a more effective leader. Sometimes it may feel like others slow us down, but in the long run they will make us so much better, faster, and stronger.

I learned to be a better speaker from someone teaching me. I learned to take risks with others when I was afraid to go alone. I gained energy and motivation from my teammates when I was too tired to go on. As a student leader, you will also need to learn, join, and build with others.

Michael Jordan, "Talent wins games, but TEAMWORK and intelligence wins championships."

Michael Jordan did not win any championships without his critical teammates and coach.

8 TEAMMATES WE NEED TO CONSTANTLY ENLIST

1. Experienced
2. Excited
3. Energized
4. Engaged

5. Encourager
6. Eager
7. Executer
8. Empathetic

8 Teammates you need to find, recruit, add, enlist!

1. EXPERIENCED

Student Leaders need to find mentors. We all do even if you are not a "Student Leader". For overall student success, we need to find some people who have experience. Someone else's experience can save you from making a mistake. Someone else's experience can help you take key steps you may not have thought about. Someone with experience can help you meet the people (connections) that will help you reach a goal.

At a summer leadership camp I attended going into my senior year, I met several students with the same goals I had. Some students shared experiences on how they had great success on AP exams and little tricks they used. Some shared how they studied for the SAT to get perfect scores. At the same camp, we were mentored by admissions officers from some of the top universities. They shared with us how to have the perfect interview and told us mistakes to avoid on our applications. The mentors showed us how to write a personal statement that helped us get accepted to the elite universities. They also showed us how to apply to scholarships and win so we could attend the university for FREE.

2. Excited

We all need the excited to "join in" friend. This friend can help you feel motivated on the days that you don't. This friend can help you stay up all night on an important project when you would have given up before you finished. The excited friend can help you join that club you feel nervous about and may even run for an officer position in the club so that you do not have to do it alone. They also may just support you as a sidekick for those times when you really just need that extra friend. The key thing they may say is "Join me" or "I'll join you".

3. Energized

Energized friends generate energy on their own. Sometimes you find a friend that lacks energy and they suck all your energy away. The energized friend does the opposite. They give you energy. They can come into a group and just by being there everyone will absorb some energy. This is also something you can learn from your friends that give the energy. When you meet them, it is always like you are meeting your best friend. They have a smile and body language that just gives you energy. One of the hardest parts about being a leader is trying to give others energy. Add friends that bring energy so you won't have to energize them and they can help you energize others.

4. Engaged

Engaged friends keep you on task. Engaged friends make you feel that they are on the team. Engaged friends make you feel like they are actively helping. Non engaged friends are quickly distracted and quick to give up on a project. Every minute that someone is engaged they are more invested in the goal. As a student leader, you have to keep everyone engaged, but with every person who is engaged on their own, this tends to be easier. When most of the group is engaged, it helps create a momentum of engagement.

5. Encouraging

Encouraging friends will help you overcome the mistakes and obstacles ahead of you. Similar to an engaged friend, but always positive. An encouraging friend will help you when you are feeling down. Encouraging friends and teammates provide that little boost of morale. Encouraging friends will make the team feel like one happy unit.

6. Eager

Eager friends want to be a part of the mission. Eager friends want to compete and win and want to put in the extra effort required. Eager friends don't require extra energy to get them on board with a project because they are already eager to be involved. Sometimes the hardest part about being a leader is trying to get someone who is not eager to get involved. Eager people jump right in without much recruiting and volunteer on projects.

7. Executor

Executer type friends make finishing a project a priority. Executors will help keep the group focused on the important things for the win. Many of the other characteristics listed above are very positive, but an executor can be a little ruthless. Not everyone will like executors, but they do get results. They will not have a problem making a decision and they don't have to be the leader, but often can take the lead. They just want to win. As the great thinker DJ Khaled says, "All I do is WIN."

8. Empathetic

Empathetic friends make sure that everyone is staying happy and doesn't get their feelings hurt. Especially if you are the one being the executor you want to have people like this around you. This person may not be empathetic towards the members in the group, but they may be empathetic towards a cause. I met a girl at one school who was so empathetic towards the students that had been bullied that she created a club to help students who had been bullied. They even raised money to bring me in to do a school assembly and some special leadership training for the club she had started.

We all need help as a student leader. I can go on and on about how sponsors, coordinators, teachers, coaches, teammates, mentors, and other students have helped me in just about every successful part of my life. You need to add all 8 kinds of people to make yourself the best student leader you can be.

Overtime/Homework (Take Action)

Write down the name of a person for each of the Characteristics and schedule a meeting. Ask them to join your team. Tell them why it is important. Then together go and make the world a better place.

1. Experienced _____
2. Excited _____
3. Energized _____
4. Engaged _____
5. Encourager _____
6. Eager _____
7. Executor _____
8. Empathetic _____

YOU WILL GO FAR AS A STUDENT LEADER! GET THE TEAMMATES TO HELP YOU GO FAR!

Remember you are a Champion Student Leader. It's GAMETIME!

NOTES

topschoolspeakers.com

topschoolspeakers.com

Scan the QR Code to Become a Certified Student Leader

CHAPTER 6

STUDENT LEADERSHIP INVEST

Jonathan Medina - "There is always a way to Win! Invest in yourself to find the way to Victory. Invest in your Student Leadership!"

Investing vs Spending

Investing is to put something in to get something even better out later. Spending is to use up without getting something better. If I give you $20 and you give me back $30 that was a good investment of my $20. If I give you $20 and you give me back $10 that was a bad investment. This same concept works in so many other things besides money.

When we put money in banks, they invest the money we give them and make more money. The same can work with our minds, body, and soul. We can invest now to become a better student leader tomorrow and in the future.

Knowing what the difference between INVESTING and spending is important because you only have 4 years of high school. You will only have 4-5 years of college. You have limited amounts of time, money, influence, etc.. You have to learn to use your time wisely and invest it instead of spending time on wrong or ineffective things.

People will try to tell you that you are not good enough. People will try and tell you that you may not be smart enough, that you may not have the experience, or even that you don't have the talent. People will try and tell you that you are not strong, pretty, handsome, fast, etc... They will try and say that you are not enough.

You are enough, but you must invest in finding the way. Student Leadership is all about finding a way.

Mark Cuban, "Because if you're prepared and you know what it takes, it's not a risk. You just have to figure out how to get there. There is always a way to get there."

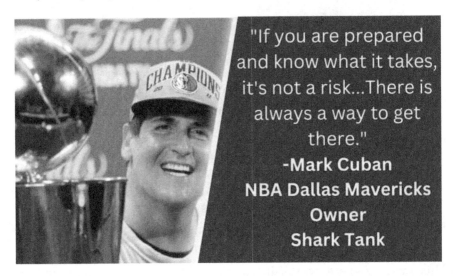

"If you are prepared and know what it takes, it's not a risk...There is always a way to get there."
-Mark Cuban
NBA Dallas Mavericks Owner
Shark Tank

Invest in Yourself! Invest in a Coach!

I can still hear my college coach giving me instructions before the biggest games. I can still remember the tips I was given that made me 10x better. I remember small and quick tips that would have huge results against my opponent. My coaches helped me change my diet so that I could quickly get bigger, faster, and stronger.

I can still hear my academic coaches who showed me a better way to study. I can remember my writing coaches who showed me how to write the perfect college essay. I can remember my SAT coach showing me how to approach the test and increase hundreds of points between tests.

I had coaches that helped me perfect my application so I could get into the top colleges.

Bill Gates, "Surround yourself with people who challenge you, teach you, and push you to be your best self."

All of my biggest and most important jumps in skills came from the advice of my coaches. Always remember you can make big and fast improvements by investing in top coaches. Invest in yourself by surrounding yourself with the right people. You need your coaches investing in you. At conferences make sure to network and meet with other student leaders that are on a mission to change the world just like you.

Invest in You! Invest Time!

Tik toc, tik toc, tik toc....We all have the same amount of time in the day. Some people are spending time and some people are investing time. The difference between spending and investing is that good investments will bring you better things in the future.

There is a Lion inside you, but you need to invest time to bring the Lion out.

You will have to make some serious choices as you grow as a Student Leader. I want you to know that the Lion Student Leader is inside you, but you will need to invest time in order to grow into the lion.

Coaches will shorten the amount of time by making every second you train more valuable. Coaches make every effort you put in your efforts more effective. Investing time, effort, and money in coaches helps you achieve your goals quicker, better, smarter.

Steph Curry shoots so good because he has spent so much time working on his shooting skills. He has the best coaches and they put in a ton of time. He has had to make serious choices about how he invests his time in order to invest the time to shoot over and over.

In the same way, as a student leader, you need to invest your time into reading books, watching leadership videos, and joining groups of other leaders. Invest time in learning to become a better public speaker. Invest time in building your team around you.

If you are not using your time to grow as a student leader, you are spending it. Make sure you either invest or spend your time wisely. Be sure to invest as much time as possible into growing your leadership by going to camps/conferences, writing down your goals, and learning the skills. You are a champion and you have a lion inside. Invest the time to bring it out.

Invest in You! Invest Resources!

You have 24 hours. You have money or you can raise money. You have friends/teammates/and others in your groups, clubs, and teams. You have supporters. You have technology. You have a dream, vision, and passion. You have energy.

Use everything you have to accomplish your positive dreams and goals. INVEST

Overtime/Homework (Take Action)

How have you invested good time and energy in the past as a student leader?

_____

_____

What are some mistakes (spending) you have made with time and energy as a student leader?

_____

_____

How can you invest your summer time instead of spending your summer time as a student leader?

_____

_____

Who are some coaches that you can Invest your time and learn from now?

_____

_____

INVEST IN STUDENT LEADERSHIP! INVEST IN YOUR FUTURE! INVEST IN YOUR INFLUENCE AND IMPACT!

Remember you are a Champion Student Leader. It's GAMETIME!

NOTES

topschoolspeakers.com

topschoolspeakers.com

Scan the QR Code to Become a Certified Student Leader

CHAPTER 7
STUDENT LEADERSHIP MEASURE

Jonathan Medina "Student Leaders Measure Success and Clearly see success"

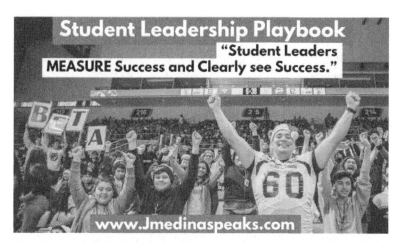

Muhammad Ali "The Greatest" - "I don't count my sit-ups. I only start counting when it starts hurting because they're the only ones that count. That's what makes you a champion."

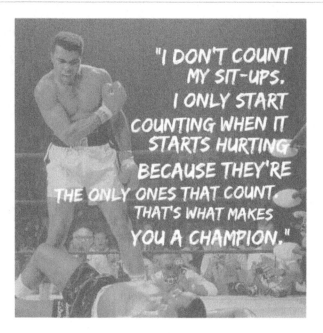

I love that quote from Muhammad Ali because so many of the things in student leadership are going to hurt. You will have to sacrifice personal goals. You will have to put in lots of hours. You will have to gain new skills. You will have to work with coaches and mentors to teach you. I am talking to you about measuring many things, but only you know what is in your heart. Nobody on the outside can measure your heart.

You will need to measure your progress toward your successful achievement of your goals. Start to count how many hurting sit ups it will take for you to accomplish your goals. If you want to go to a certain college you need to know the GPA required for admission. You will need to know the SAT score required. If you are in a competition you need to know what kind of score you need to get from the judges.

Are you an effective public speaker? Are you able to persuade others with your communication? Do you have an ability to recruit people to join your club? Has your club membership grown? Do you feel you have grown as a leader?

The only way for you to know if you are growing as a leader is to measure your progress toward achieving your goals for success.

When I became class president in my sophomore grade year, our sponsor started our first meeting by reviewing the class financial status. She told me how much money the class had earned from fundraisers. She estimated how much money we would need to raise over the next two years to host class events and celebrations. She told me how many students had been attending class meetings and how many to expect at future meetings. Because this wise lady had measured how successful our class fundraisers had been in the past, I was able to see how hard we would need to work to raise enough money to do all the things we hoped and we had a long way to go!

I am forever grateful that she showed me how important it is to measure your progress toward achieving your goals. We planned our strategy and identified important achievement measurements. From that moment forward, I began to use her strategy of measuring achievement in all aspects of my student leadership.

In second grade, Dr. Laura Sheneman taught me the importance of always being steps ahead. She showed me the game of chess. In order to achieve success in chess you must be steps ahead. You must always be aware of your current position and the final goals.

Do you plan on going to a leadership conference? How much money do you need to raise to take your entire leadership team? How many have been going to conferences in the past? Have you improved in a competition that you work on? What are the important measurable results you can begin to track to ensure success in your organization or team?

As a student athlete, measuring myself against other top athletes allowed me to see that I had a chance to play college football because I could see that I was not far from being strong and fast enough for someone my size. I imagined what schools I would like to play for and I looked at the players on scholarship. I noticed that I was a little undersized so I needed to make up for my lack of size by being faster, stronger, and have better grades than those on scholarship. Measuring and working to increase my strength and speed allowed me to find success and achieve my goal of playing college football.

Do you compete in something where you have a weakness? How can you overcome the weakness by improving other areas?

Going back to my experience as class president. Measuring success also made me feel good as we were growing in success. Our student leadership team continued to grow and I kept seeing how much improvement we made to the club. Measuring success helped me to see the vision as we tracked closer and closer to the final goal of raising the money and our class creating a legacy. Measuring our achievement toward our goal helped me to see that some decisions did not help the club or even hurt the club. I made mistakes and I observed others mistakes. I was aware that if I was not leading effectively it was possible to leave the organization (my class) worse than when i started. Measuring success helped everyone to see how each person's effort was helping us get closer to achieving our goals. There are so many benefits to measuring success. Someday when you are older I want you to look back and see how much growth you made as a student leader. Measure where you are now and where you want to be someday. Measuring will help you identify the effectiveness of your student leadership.

Something only you can measure for yourself.

Your potential can't be measured because no one can see inside your heart. No one knows all the decisions that you consider in your mind. Only you can see what is in your heart. Only you can truly measure the effort and effectiveness you are capable of accomplishing. Be a Champion Student Leader inside and out. Be a Champion Student Leader in your heart.

Zig Ziglar, "Success is not measured by what you do compared to what somebody else does. Success is measured by what you do compared to what you are capable of doing."

Bonus Tip

An important additional thing I want you to measure is every challenge or obstacle you have overcome. A few years ago my mom got into some trouble and I suddenly had to take care of all my siblings. Overnight I was a parent to 4 kids. I was trying to seem strong, but on the inside I was very scared and very worried about how I was going to do it. A great friend and second mom, Laura, told me she could see that I was nervous so she gave me some great advice. I was supposed to be mentoring her children and helping them prepare for the student leadership camps I was running. Her team invited me to a planning meeting where they had a huge goal of sending nearly 200 kids to camp. I was supporting them but I was the one who ended up being supported.

Laura told me to remember all the things I had overcome in the past and that I could overcome this also. Measure and take note of all the things that you have overcome. The obstacles you overcome now will give you confidence to overcome challenges in the future. Every bit of growth you measure now can help you have confidence in your future.

In college I helped to raise nearly $200,000 in scholarships for future students. I could never have raised so much without the lessons from high school fundraising. Also helped to raise approximately $250,000 for student leadership organizations. I could not have done that without all the lessons learned by measuring success & overcoming obstacles.

Imagine right now how everything you have learned and overcome can help you do something positive in the future. Imagine how you can use the skills you are learning to change the world. Go and be a successful leader.

Booker T Washington, "If you truly want to measure the success of a man, you do not measure it by a position he has achieved, but by the obstacles he has overcome.

Overtime/Homework (Take Action)

5 Things Every Student Leader can/should measure.

1. How much time do I invest in myself (Books, Podcast, Self development)
2. How much time do I invest in the others in my group, club, organization, and team?
3. How many leadership camps, conferences, or conventions do I go to each year?
4. How many other students do I recruit to join groups, clubs, organizations, and teams?
5. How many other students do you recruit to go to leadership camps, conferences, or conventions each year?

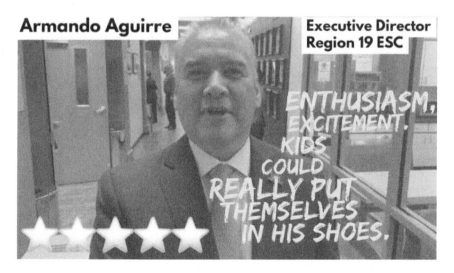

STUDENT LEADERS MEASURE PROGRESS!
STUDENT LEADERS MEASURE SUCCESS!

Remember you are a Champion Student Leader. It's GAMETIME!

NOTES

Scan the QR Code to Become a Certified Student Leader

CHAPTER 8
STUDENT LEADERSHIP ENGAGE

Jonathan Medina - "Where student leadership engagement goes, entire organization success follows."

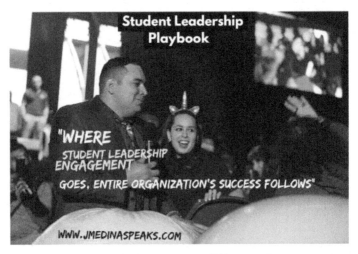

Have you ever noticed that success follows whatever activities you invest or spend the most time in? As a Student Leader you often have to make a decision on what activities and what organizations you can be truly engaged in. You will experience more success in the organization to which you devote the most time and energy.

There is an old parable of two wolves. Usually the story is told with one wolf representing Anger and the other a positive emotion such as Compassion. The story goes that the wolves go to battle each day with one another. Every day the wolves battle, one wins over the other. As the wolves grow, one wolf begins to win more often than the other. Eventually the one wolf is stronger than the other and always wins. Which is the wolf that becomes stronger? The wolf that eats more grows bigger and stronger and has success.

I tell that story to say that whatever activities we want to be successful in need to be fed with the nutrition of Engagement. When we are engaged in activities we become successful.

WHAT ACTIVITIES, SKILLS, & MINDSETS WILL YOU FEED?

The chorus of a song written by John Mayer goes, "I keep on waiting, waiting, waiting for the world to change." A Student Leader does not wait for the world to change. A Student Leader engages and sets out to change the world. A Student Leader engages other leaders and starts a movement to better the world. A Student Leader sees a need on campus and recruits/engages others to develop strategies to address the problem. A Student Leader does not wait.

What if Christopher Columbus had stayed at home? What if JK Rowlings had never written the Harry Potter Series? What if Dr. King had not shared his dream? What if Michael Jordan had not tried to fly?

What if, what if, what if???

I love what the Quarterback of the Seattle Seahawks says about "what ifs." Russell Wilson says, "Always give your best effort so your memories won't be filled with: would-haves, could-haves, should-haves, and what-ifs." Best way to not have "what ifs" is to give your best effort (Engagement).

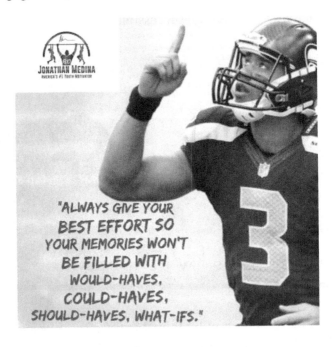

Abraham Lincoln "Things may come to those who wait, but only the things left by those who hustle."

Lincoln understood that if you want to be a successful student leader you need to engage. You can't just be waiting for success in your organization. You must engage in planning, recruiting, and growing.

Overtime/Homework (Take Action)

What are 3 ways you plan on engaging success as a student leader?

How can you improve by engaging your student leadership abilities?

STUDENT LEADERS ENGAGE & CHANGE THE WORLD.

Remember you are a Champion Student Leader. It's GAMETIME!

Final Message
I am so proud of you!

Choose!
Commit!
Coaching!
Community!
Create!

GAMETIME

Goals
Attitude
Mindset
Embody
Teamwork
Invest
Measure
Engage

Congrats!

You have chosen to become a student leader that is growing. Congrats you have committed to excellence. Congrats you have decided to be coachable! You have come together with me, my team, and all the student leaders my team works with. Congrats on creating a new and better you. You are the new breed of student leader.

Many people today say so many negative things about the student leaders of today, but I believe in you. I believe you are a Champion! I believe you are the new breed of student leaders that will take your organization, your team, and the world to new heights.

Thank you for investing your time and energy in reading this book.

Let it be your playbook for making the world a better place.

topschoolspeakers.com

Scan the QR Code to Become a
Certified Student Leader

Remember you are a Champion Student Leader. It's GAMETIME!

NOTES

#1 Best Selling Book

Thank you Launch Team for helping me get to #1. Thousands sold!

Book Launch Stats

#1 Children's Book Social Emotional Issues

#1 Children's Book Leadership

#1 Teen Book Social Emotional Issues

#1 Children's Book on Friendships

#23 Motivational Book All Ages

Top Rated Student Leadership Book 40+ 5 Star Reviews

Thank you…

Art, Brenda, Greek, Leisha, Noemi, Diane, Tewell, Bro John, Bailey, Crystal M, Noelia, Felipe, Veronica, Kristy, Germard, George, Jozabad, David, Susie, Fernando, Bubb, Zach, Melissa, Jessica, Yaw, Lucio, RJ. Plus many more!

topschoolspeakers.com

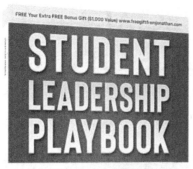

Join the Student Leadership Success Challenge!
$100 FREE!

READ THIS FIRST

Just to say thanks for buying my book, I would like to give you the Challenge 100% FREE!

Get Certificate of completion for Resume!

TO DOWNLOAD GO TO:

www.FreeGiftFromJonathan.com

topschoolspeakers.com

SPECIAL $1000 FREE BONUS GIFT FOR YOU!

To help you achieve more success, there are **FREE BONUS RESOURCES** for you at:

Get your 8 FREE in-depth training videos sharing

- How top achieving student leaders
- Attract more followers!
- Increase influence!
- Lead & Achieve more Goals!
- Create Movements & Go Viral!
- Plus Secret Bonuses.

www.FreeGiftFromJonathan.com

topschoolspeakers.com

Student Success Playbook © Copyright <<2020>> Jonathan Medina

All rights reserved. No part of this publication may be reproduced, distributed or transmitted in any form or by any means, including photocopying, recording, or other electronic or mechanical methods, without the prior written permission of the publisher, except in the case of brief quotations embodied in critical reviews and certain other noncommercial uses permitted by copyright law.

Although the author and publisher have made every effort to ensure that the information in this book was correct at press time, the author and publisher do not assume and hereby disclaim any liability to any party for any loss, damage, or disruption caused by errors or omissions, whether such errors or omissions result from negligence, accident, or any other cause.

Adherence to all applicable laws and regulations, including international, federal, state and local governing professional licensing, business practices, advertising, and all other aspects of doing business in the US, Canada or any other jurisdiction is the sole responsibility of the reader and consumer.

Neither the author nor the publisher assumes any responsibility or liability whatsoever on behalf of the consumer or reader of this material. Any per-ceived slight of any individual or organization is purely unintentional.

The resources in this book are provided for informational purposes only and should not be used to replace the specialized training and professional judgment of a health care or mental health care professional.

Neither the author nor the publisher can be held responsible for the use of the information provided within this book. Please always consult a trained professional before making any decision regarding treatment of yourself or others.

For more information, email jonathan@jmedinaspeaks.com

ISBN: 9798693072817

Biggest Thank you to my #1 Supporter. Thank you to my #1 Person. My #1 Motivation. My Greatest Leadership Coach! Thank you Kristina Medina and our Family!

Thank You FCA

My life changed because of FCA.

My leadership grew because of FCA. My Impact was molded by FCA. FCA gave me the Vision. "1st and Last!"

Thank you!

Buddle, Guzman, Dave K, Nigel, Jan, Sam O, Liz, Gina, Dan Bishop, Robbie G, D Brittain, Don, Kerry, Barney, Nathan, Jenn, Roel, Jimmy C, Flaherty, Wes, Pat, Jimmy P, Bill, Peter, Able, Lisa, Santiago, Mikado, Greek, Jeff M, Hoffler, Anderson, Corbin, K Washington, Benavides, Josephe, Volpe, Jobe, Jorge, Isaiah, Amico, Chauncey, Alex, Kristen, Dan, Ben, Sandy, Galvan, Flinn, Johnsons, Sparks, Keath, Katie, Ryner, Elliff, Boggus, Urbis, Murphy, Snell, Duffy, Quisenberry, Burke, Bro Frank, SWK, PJ, Elliott, Farris, Duncan, Lackey, Whisenant, Bob, ICC, Hinojosa, Wade, Joe, Sales, Garcia, Tip, House, Starkey, Mr. G, Dahlberg, Schuster, Dizdar, Carrillo, Joey, Mata, Lougheed, Abram, Hornberger, Kohler, Parsons, Keith, Ford, Honea, Lara, Poynter, Infante, Bo, Clarence, Gomez, Gomez, Carroll, Kristen, Jenni, RJ, Abe, Gonzalez, Phylli, Crystal, Mr. V, Melizza, Shears, Moore, Hesterberg, Gonzalo, Samaniego, Cabrera, Solis, Williams, Castros, Murphy, Huddleston, Billy G, Wilde, Sarah, Darrell, Starla, Gray, Phipps, Palmos, Mark, Kreters, Molina, Manny, Franks, Johnsons, Brown, Wilson, plus so many more!!!

Thank you Rio Hondo! I went to about 18 Different schools, but I always claim Rio Hondo as Home. The community & people of Rio Hondo helped me start in Leadership!

Cortez, Guzman, Buddle, Stephenson, De La Rosa, Cavazos, Gomez, Rosales, Gonzalez, King, Jauregui, Sauceda Family, Sauceda, Medieros Family, Alfaro Family, Atkinson Family, McKinney, Savage, Garza Family, Chauncey, Liz, RJ, Cristela, Oscar, Tommy, Jeremiah, Jaymes, Aaron, Eric, Caleb, Uribe, Herrera, Molina Family, Montez, Carlos, Alvarez, James Family, Blue, Kretz, Lewis, Marroquin, Rangel, Robledo, Salinas, Tuffy, Dustin, Brian, Eddie, Jaime, Robbie, Gantt, Ryan, Roland, Jeremy, Adan, Leo, Roy, Chapa, Eloy, Boen, Divina, Veronica, Karissa, Thianna, Jasmine, Boris, Alaniz, Aguirre, Cowan, Everett, Hinojosa, Serna, Ortega, Ramirez, Rodriquez, Waters, Vineyard, Mesa.

Thank you Georgetown Football
4 Years for 40

Coach Kelly, Coach Sgarlatta, Coach Dunley, DEmir, Ike, Baker, Kenny, Bassuener, Fajgenbaum, Barbiaz, Willie, Dennis, Cassidy, Houghton, Kinnan, Lane, Buzbee, Umar, Conyers, Rau, Tmack, Cooper, Craft, Dito, Tavarez, Stephen, Paulus, coffman, Amaro, Matheny, Moses, Brooks, Chudi, Grubb, Mosle, Cherundolo, Rehwinkle, Osterhout, Beacher, Bowe, Josephs, Myers, Collin, lloyd, Nnamdi, Tomlinson, Hussey, Ataefiok, Keerome, Fleet, Parrish, Antiko, Semler, Hollowman, Isdaner, Phil, Cosgrove, Kayal, jayah, shabazz, Simmons, Ty, Brock, Moore, and other Football Hoyas.

HOYA SAXA #CuraPersonalis Georgetown/College

Ben, Dan, Alex, Kinnan, Andrew, James, Dave, Adam, Hector, Ramses, Kristen, Jenn, Erica, Sandy, Kortney, Johnny, Adrienne, Edgar, Pena, Josh, Berto, Alejandro, Lorina, Aida, Brenda, Jessica, Paola, Cassie, De Man, Shaw, Sesma, Eronini, Yu, Juan, Karina, Yasmin, Kelsey, Bonnie, Vezina, Mow, Vargas, Haskins, Marco, Ale, Justin, Tommy, Oscar & Amber Castro, Cassie, Lorena, Bishops, De Man, Kemp, Schvitz,

topschoolspeakers.com

THE IDEAL PROFESSIONAL SPEAKER FOR YOUR NEXT EVENT!

TO CONTACT OR BOOK JONATHAN TO SPEAK:
(832) 713-0296
jonathan@jmedinaspeaks.com
topschoolspeakers.com/jmedinaspeaks

LEADERSHIP NOTES

#1 Best Selling Book

Thank you Launch Team for helping me get to #1. Thousands sold!

Book Launch Stats

#1 Children's Book Social Emotional Issues

#1 Children's Book Leadership

#1 Teen Book Social Emotional Issues

#1 Children's Book on Friendships

#23 Motivational Book All Ages

Top Rated Student Leadership Book 40+ 5 Star Reviews

Thank you...

Art, Brenda, Greek, Leisha, Noemi, Diane, Tewell, Bro John, Bailey, Crystal M, Noelia, Felipe, Veronica, Kristy, Germard, George, Jozabad, David, Susie, Fernando, Bubb, Zach, Melissa, Jessica, Yaw, Lucio, RJ. Plus many more!

topschoolspeakers.com

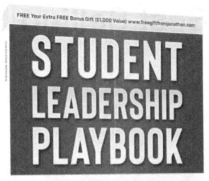

Join the Student Leadership Success Challenge!

~~$100~~ FREE!

READ THIS FIRST

Just to say thanks for buying my book,

I would like to give you the

Challenge 100% FREE!

Get Certificate of completion for Resume!

TO DOWNLOAD GO TO:

www.FreeGiftFromJonathan.com

topschoolspeakers.com

SPECIAL $1000 FREE BONUS GIFT FOR YOU!

To help you achieve more success, there are
FREE BONUS RESOURCES for you at:

Get your 8 FREE in-depth training videos sharing

- How top achieving student leaders
- Attract more followers!
- Increase influence!
- Lead & Achieve more Goals!
- Create Movements & Go Viral!
- Plus Secret Bonuses.

www.FreeGiftFromJonathan.com

Made in the USA
Middletown, DE
01 April 2025